What Just Happened To Me?

a Bible study for new believers

Regina McCollam

Published by:
SOUNDS OF THE NATIONS
PO Box 7216
Round Rock, TX 78683

Cover design by Regina McCollam
Cover Painting by Lyn Lasneski – www.lynlasneski.info
Editing and interior design by Regina McCollam

Printed in the USA

ISBN-13: 978-1544067223
ISBN-10: 1544067224

Table of Contents

Introduction

I hope that your introduction to Jesus has so rocked your world that you are truly asking, "What just happened to me?" Becoming a born-again believer in Jesus Christ, also known as a Christian, is no small occurrence. There is a literal transformation that has taken place within you, and the more you understand it, the more free and powerful your new life with Christ will be.

In this beginner-level study, we will first answer the question of what did happen the moment you acknowledged Jesus Christ as your Savior. Then we will talk about a few of the basic yet amazing things you have available to you that will help you grow as a Christian.

We will look at *a lot* of Bible verses. Look up each Scripture. Take your time to thoughtfully answer each question that is printed in bold font. Space is given for you to write out your answers. Let the truth of each verse sink into your spirit before you move on to the next one. The questions are designed to be pondered. Like a news reporter, if you will take the time to ask questions of each Bible text, you will uncover more understanding than if you simply read, answer, and move on.

An important part of becoming a strong Christian is letting God speak to you through His Word, the Bible. This study presumes that you, the reader, have stepped into relationship with Jesus Christ as Savior and choose to believe the Bible is the Word of God. Without that belief, these questions and answers will have a lesser impact. It is by faith the Word releases its power into your life.

Some would argue that the Bible was written by men and therefore not trustworthy. We will talk about that more in depth in lesson two. For now, I want to share with you that given all the arguments out there, I have chosen to believe the Bible is the written Word of God. I believe every word in its original composition was intentionally placed there by God for a reason, and so I continuously ask God, "What are you saying to me through this Bible verse?" Even though I am not perfect, and my understanding of the Bible is not complete and sometimes even off, and man's translations of the original manuscripts now and then misrepresent, the Scripture itself has never let me down. Indeed, it has become my closest friend, strongest ally, wisest counselor, and most faithful comforter. I've decided that if I am going to make a mistake as a Christian it will be in believing the Bible too much and trusting God too completely. It is with this heart that I offer the thoughts of the following pages to you.

If you are not yet sure what you believe about the Bible's accuracy and truth, that's okay. You have the right to weigh carefully what you choose to believe. For now, will you commit to continue on into the study with an open heart, answering each question according to what you read in the Scriptures and setting aside for now preconceived ideas or thoughts about God? Let the Bible speak for itself while you listen with an open heart.

In the center columns throughout each lesson are listed additional Scripture references that apply to the topic being discussed. Look those up if you want more information. I encourage you to pray before reading the Word. Ask God to show you things about Himself and about yourself each time you venture into it.

My passion is for you to know God more with each turn of the page and also for you to be equipped with enough understanding to get your feet solidly on the ground as a new Christian. When I read over these lessons, I get excited for you and the life in Christ that you are just beginning. Knowing God is a lifelong journey; there is so much more to discover about Him than you will find in these few pages, but let the journey begin.

1

What Just Happened To Me?

Something really big just happened to you. It's powerful, and it changes everything. You just became a born-again Christian by confessing that Jesus Christ is Lord and by believing in your heart that God raised Him from the dead. Jesus is now the ever-present, acting Lord of your life. Welcome to the kingdom of God! In this lesson are a few thoughts from the Bible that are important for you to know concerning what happened when you accepted Jesus' invitation to live closely in relationship with Him.

If you haven't read the introduction, please go back and do so. It contains some instructions for how to get the most out of this study for yourself. I'll say it again. Something really big just happened to you. The more you know about it and the more you believe it, the more joyous and freeing your new walk with Christ will be. Ready? Let's find out what just happened to you.

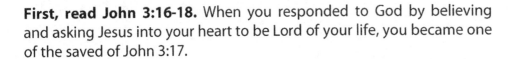

First, read John 3:16-18. When you responded to God by believing and asking Jesus into your heart to be Lord of your life, you became one of the saved of John 3:17.

Read that verse again.

Romans 5:8-10
1 John 4:9-10

Now read verse 18 slowly.

Matthew 18:14
2 Peter 3:9

Have *you* believed in Jesus?

According to verse 18, if you believe in Jesus, what is now true of you?

What two things are true of the one who believes in Jesus according to verse 16?

Acts 2:21

Of course, this doesn't mean that your mortal body will never die; but for those who believe in Jesus, eternal life in heaven awaits when life on earth is through, and current life on earth can now be the abundant life that Jesus came to give—yes, even in the worst of circumstances.

John 11:25-26
Hebrews 9:27

John 10:10

So, you are now one of the saved! Saved from what?

Look at Matthew 1:21. In this passage, an angel is telling Joseph about Jesus, the baby Mary is going to have. **What does this verse say Jesus will save us from?**

1 John 5:17 tells us what sin is: "all wrong-doing is sin." One of the original definitions of sin in the Bible is "to miss the mark" in your relationship with God. Another definition is "a violation of divine law in thought or deed." There are many passages in Scripture that give details about specific things that God calls sin such as murder, lying, adultery, etc. Let's not get caught up in trying to compile a complete list of sins or even in trying to figure out if one sin is worse than another. All wrongdoing is sin, and all wrongdoing misses the mark in your relationship with God.

Read the following verses. Note in each one what God has done with your sin now that you are saved and Jesus is present as the head of your life.

Psalm 103:12

Hebrews 10:17

1 John 1:9

So, now all your sins are forgiven and forgotten. What about tomorrow? How will you live this new life tomorrow? How will you keep from your old lifestyle of sin? Jeremiah 17:9 tells us a man's heart is deceitful above all things. It says there is no cure for the wickedness of our hearts. Verse one even says sin is engraved with an iron tool on the tablets of our hearts. It would seem there is no hope for us to change. No hope for us to live a righteous life that would please God. No hope except for two important details.

1 John 3:4
James 4:17
Galatians 5:14
Galatians 5:19-25

Matthew 22:36-40

Psalm 103:1-14
Isaiah 38:17
Isaiah 43:25
Romans 4:7-8
1 John 1:7

Hebrews 10:14-23

1 John 2:1

1. A REALLY BIG PROMISE

These next verses for you to look up are about the covenant promise of rescue that God made to the Israelites. A promise of a savior was already made in Genesis 3:15; and Galatians 3:16 clearly tells us that savior is Jesus Christ. Throughout all Old Testament history, people were not able to keep their commitment of obedience to God, emphasizing mankind's need for a savior and supernatural assistance; but now, through Jesus, something has changed.

Read these verses and list what God has promised. List every detail. Especially notice what happens to your wicked heart. In each of these verses, "I" refers to God.

Jeremiah 24:7, 31:31-33

Ezekiel 11:19-20, 36:25-27

What happened to your wicked heart?

Besides giving you a new heart, what else does Ezekiel 36:27 say God put within you?

According to this verse, what is His Spirit doing within you?

We were all once full of all kinds of sin, but when the kindness and love of God showed up in the form of Jesus Christ, He saved us. Because of

Genesis 3:15
Galatians 3:16

Genesis 22:18
Romans 1:16
Acts 28:28
The promises of God are extended to all nationalities.

Ezekiel 36:26-36
(Imagine that your life is the land described in these verses.)
John 3:3-7

Hebrews 10:16-18
Romans 6:6-7

2 Corinthians 5:17

John 14:16-20
Romans 8:5-9
1 Corinthians. 3:16
Ephesians 1:13-14

1 Peter 2:10
Colossians 1:21-23

His mercy, God washed away our sins, giving us a new birth and new life through the Holy Spirit.

2. A HELPER

That last verse you read promised that God would put His Spirit within the believer. Let's take a closer look at what the Holy Spirit, who is now in you, is doing in you.

Look up the following verses. List the other names the Holy Spirit is known by. A person's nickname can tell you something of what that person is like.

John 14:16-17

John 14:26 (Jesus is speaking.)

John 15:26 (Jesus is speaking.)

John 16:13-15 (Jesus is speaking.)

Think for a minute about these qualities of Holy Spirit. This is who Holy Spirit is for you. What a tremendous gift God has given us in sending the Holy Spirit to us.

Read these verses a second time and note what the Holy Spirit's job is in each reference. Do the same for the two additional verses.

John 15:26
Mark 13:10-11
Acts 1:2
Acts 1:8
Romans 5:5
Romans 15:13
Ephesians 1:13-14
2 Peter 1:21
1 Cor. 2:10-13

John 14:16-17

John 14:26

John 16:13-15

Romans 8:26-27

Ephesians 3:16 (Apostle Paul is speaking.)

When Romans 8:26 tells us the Holy Spirit is interceding for you, it literally means He goes to the Father on your behalf and consults with Father on what is best for you in this moment. Be encouraged to know that in your new Christian life, you are never alone. The Holy Spirit is in you and always ready to help you.

I want you to look up one more word of encouragement. **Turn to 2 Corinthians 5:17. How does God see you now?**

Recalling all you have discovered in this lesson, what happened to you when you believed in Jesus?   Ephesians 4:22-32

Oh, friend in Christ, there is so much more to learn about your new walk with Jesus. With a clean slate, the Word by your side, and the Holy Spirit in you, may you grow in grace and in the knowledge of our Lord and Savior Jesus Christ and may you fall more in love with Him and His loving ways every day.

2

Is Anybody Hungry?

A human's body needs food and water to live. So does the spiritual part of you. What is the food and water that your spirit needs? In Matthew 4:4, Jesus said man shall not live by bread alone but by every word that comes from the mouth of God. Ephesians 5:26 speaks of the "water of the word." The Bible is one way God speaks to you; it is food and water to you. You need it to be healthy in your new life with God. Let's spend some time exploring what makes the Bible so important to you.

Take the time to look up each Scripture. Also notice the context of each reference you look up. Context, simply defined, is the paragraph(s) before and after the verse at which you are looking. Knowing what surrounds a verse helps you interpret meaning more accurately.

Did you pray before beginning today's study? Ask God to show you things about Himself and about yourself.

Throughout this study, you will encounter different names for the Bible: Word of God, Scripture, commandments, precepts, prophecy, perfect law. Know that generally they all are referring to God's written Word, the Bible.

First, let's see what the Bible says about itself. Who wrote the Bible and from whom did the authors receive inspiration?

2 Peter 1:20-21

Acts 1:16
Acts 28:25
1Cor. 2:12-13

2 Timothy 3:16

The word "God-breathed" in 2 Timothy 3:16 means inspired by God. The Holy Spirit breathed the character of God into the written Word. **According to this verse, how much of Scripture is inspired by God?**

This doesn't mean that God took ahold of the writer's hand and forcibly caused him to write out exactly what He wanted to say. No, the beauty of the Scripture is God's partnership with humans in its writing. And yes, when you consider the deep imperfections of the human race, it is a wonder that the Bible is so excellently put together. Yet, it is such a fantastic piece of literature that it will take you a lifetime to fully explore it and to experience its power.

As a Christian now, you will have an opinion about the value of the Bible in your life. Is it the Word of God or not? Is all of it inspired and meant to be accepted as holy and true, or just parts of it? I have chosen to believe it all, every word of it. I can testify that because of my unwavering confidence that the Bible is God-breathed and full of the Holy Spirit, the Scriptures have become living and active in my life. They are my closest friend, my wisest counselor, my source of answers, and my greatest comfort next to God himself. What are *you* going to believe about Scripture? Let's learn a little more about it before you answer.

What is Scripture good for? What does it do in you and for you? In other words, why was it written?

Psalm 119:1-176

John 20:30-31

2 Timothy 3:15-17

Psalm 139:23-24

Hebrews 4:12

Ephesians 6:17
Compare responses
in Acts 2:37
and Acts 5:33

1 Peter 2:2 ("Pure spiritual milk" could also be translated as "pure milk of the word.")

Psalm 119:105

Psalm 119:130

The Bible is such a big book, and the more you dig into it, the bigger it gets. It can be a bit overwhelming to think that we can read and understand God's words. How is it possible that each one of us really can understand it and apply it to our lives regardless of who we are?

Paul spoke a prayer for Christians in Ephesians 1:17 and Colossians 1:9-12 that would extend to all believers through all time. **What did he ask for, and why did he ask for it?**

Ephesians 1:15-20

Daniel 2:22
1 Corinthians. 2:10-12
1 Corinthians. 2:16

Colossians 1:9 (Write down what this prayer asked for.)

Now make a list of why Paul prayed this Colossians prayer. What will being filled with spiritual wisdom and understanding do for you? The list begins with the words "so that" in verse 10 and continues through verse 12.

Philippians 1:9-11

1.

2.

3.

4.

5.

6.

Do you want all of this? Do you think God would answer Paul's prayer for you?

The Scriptures are an incredible gift to us from the Father. 2 Peter 1:3 even tells us that God's divine power has given us everything we need for a godly life through our knowledge of Christ. Think about that. Everything we need we have access to through understanding who Jesus is to us. The Bible is the primary source for knowing who Jesus is. Every story, every verse reveals something about Him.

Look up these next verses. Who else helps us understand what we read in the Bible; who is our teacher?

Ephesians 1:15-20

1 Corinthians 2:11-13

John 14:25-26 (This is Jesus speaking to His disciples.)

If God, through the Holy Spirit, is the one who helps us understand what the Word says, then each time we open the Bible to read or study it, we should pray. The same words Paul prayed for you, you can pray for yourself. Ask God to teach you. Ask Him to help you understand what you are reading but also to give you wisdom. Wisdom is knowing how to apply the Bible to your life—knowing how to live out what you just learned.

Compare the one who lives out or obeys God's Word to the one who doesn't in the following verses. Look closely; note the differences.

John 16:33

Psalm 119
Exodus 19:5-6
Romans 2:13
1 John 2:3-6

Matthew 7:24-27

James 1:22-25

From Matt. 7:24 and James 1:22 and 25, list exactly what it is that God wants you to do with His Word.

Proverbs 14:1
James 2:20-26

From Matt. 7:25 and James 1:25, what are the good things that happen to the one who does these things?

God is very clear that it is not by good works that you are saved—it is by believing in Jesus Christ that you are saved. Yet, the book of James tells us that faith without good works is not real faith at all—in other words, if you really love God and He is truly the Lord of your life, it will show up in the way you live your life.

John 14:15-30
Romans 4:1-5
Galatians 2:16, 20-21
Ephesians 2:8-10
Titus 3:4-8
James 2:14-26
1 John 2:3-11

Read Philippians 2:13. Who is at work in you?

What is He working in you?

"To will" in Philippians 2:13 refers to the *desire* to act according to what pleases God. "To act" or "to work" means the *ability to actually do* what pleases God. So, you see, God expects us to obey His Word, yet He is the one who gives us both the *desire* and the *ability to do* it. He knows we can't do it on our own and lovingly comes along side us with divine help.

John 14:15-17
1 Corinthians 15:9-10
Read Hebrews 13:20-21. Again, who gives you the ability to live out what you learn in the Bible? With what has He equipped you?

According to 2 Peter 1:3, where do we get everything we need to live a godly life? What does it come through?

God is looking for a full-time commitment of our bodies, souls, and spirits. But then He turns around and gives us everything we need to make and keep that commitment through our relationship with Jesus Christ. All we have to do is let Him.

According to 2 Peter 1:4, it is through Jesus and His goodness that God has made these promises to help us. **Read verse 4—what are you now able to do by believing these promises of God? What have you escaped?**

Ephesians 4:7
"Believe" is an action word. It is not just something you feel; it is something you live. Faith is a gift from God, and a measure of it has been

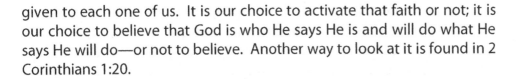

given to each one of us. It is our choice to activate that faith or not; it is our choice to believe that God is who He says He is and will do what He says He will do—or not to believe. Another way to look at it is found in 2 Corinthians 1:20.

> *For no matter how many promises God has made, they are "Yes" in Christ. And so through him the "Amen" is spoken by us to the glory of God. (NIV)*

God's promises are always "yes." It is our responsibility then to add the "amen" which means "so be it." It is our responsibility to agree with God and allow Him to do the work in our hearts.

I want you to look up one more word of encouragement concerning the Bible and you. **Read Isaiah 55:10-11. What is God's promise concerning His Word in you?**

Friend in Christ, the Bible is the Word of God—His message to you and His promises to you. Through it, He is talking to you, encouraging you, answering your questions about how to live your Christian life. Would you accept an invitation to a delicious meal wonderfully prepared by your loved one and then not eat, not savor every bite? Is anybody hungry? God has so many things to tell you. Pick up His book daily, read, listen, and eat it up.

1 Peter 1:23
Isaiah 55:1-11

3

Let's Talk

Today I want to share with you one of the basic yet most powerful aspects of your new Christian life. Prayer.

Take time to look up each answer. Please don't hurry on to the next question. Stop and think. Ask Holy Spirit for insight and to write His Word upon your heart so that you will not forget it.

What is prayer? According to Spiros Zodhiates, a Greek language expert, original words for prayer used in the New Testament mean "to meet and talk with God," and "to call upon God for aid." Prayer is simply getting together with God, speaking with Him about what is on your heart, and listening to what is on His heart. Prayer is an open communication line between us and God.

Read Matthew 6:8. What does it tell us about Father God?

If the Father knows what we need before we ask, why do we have to ask? Maybe if we look at wrong reasons to pray, we will have a clearer picture of what God's purpose is for having us pray. Read Matthew 6:5-8. This is part of what is known as "The Sermon On the Mount" where Jesus spoke for three chapters about the attitudes of our hearts as we live our lives on earth. **In verse 5, how did He say not to pray? What is not to be our reason for spending time in prayer?**

Psalm 38:9

Motive matters. Make your conversations with God about just that—a real conversation. Focus on sharing your heart and life with Father God and on seeking His counsel and will on whatever topic is on your mind. If you are thinking more about how your prayers look to others than about the one you are speaking to, maybe you are not actually speaking to God.

In verse 7, what does Jesus tell us not to do?

Matthew 6:25-33
Acts 15:8

So, what is prayer not? It is not meaningless repetition. It is not thoughtless rambling. It is not a religious ritual. Prayer is authentic communication with a real listening God.

Back to our question of why we need to ask in the first place, look at verse 6. Picture in your mind doing just what Jesus describes in this verse.

Proverbs 15:8
Psalm 38:9

Now you are alone in a private room in your heart, just you and Father God. What are you going to talk about? What is your attitude going to be as you talk? In this place alone with God, there is nothing you cannot say, nothing that needs to remain hidden. You can share your true thoughts, your questions, your experiences, your needs and desires—everything. I think that kind of relationship is one thing God is looking for by making it necessary to communicate with Him through prayer.

Matthew 14:23
Matthew 26:36-44
Mark 1:35
John 17

Did you know Jesus had to pray? While on earth He communicated with the Father by prayer the same way we do. Jesus told us that He did nothing by himself and did only what He saw His Father doing. (John 6:19-20) How did Jesus know what the Father was doing? Through prayer, Jesus asked, listened, and then did.

Read Hebrews 5:7. Why was Jesus heard when he prayed?

Sure, Jesus was heard; He's the son of God. But is anybody really listening when *you* pray? **When you pray, what is happening in heaven?**

James 5:16
Proverbs 15:29

Psalm 34:15

Psalm 145:18-19

Proverbs 21:13
Matthew 5:22-24
Mark 11:22-25
James 1:6-8

Why then does it seem at times that no one is listening? Why are prayers sometimes not responded to?

Psalm 66:17-20

Mark 11:24-25

Malachi 2:13-15

1 Peter 3:7

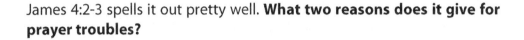

James 4:2-3 spells it out pretty well. **What two reasons does it give for prayer troubles?**

Can you see that even though sometimes things get in the way of our communication with God, it is His great pleasure and desire to respond to our prayers with good things? God is not stubborn or fickle, giving us the silent treatment when we don't do things His way. No, He has shown us exactly what we can do to open the windows of heaven over our own lives.

Read the entire parable found in Luke 18:1-8. What should you do, according to Luke 18:1, when the hindrance to your prayer is not sin or unbelief, yet an answer has not come?

James 5:16
Psalm 55:17
Romans 12:12
Ephesians 6:18

Luke 11:5-13

Is God comparing Himself to the unrighteous judge or showing how He is different? How so?

Psalm 116:5
Isaiah 41:10

What is God asking of us through this parable?

1 Thessalonians 5:17

James 5:16 tells us the prayer of a righteous man is powerful and effective. Let's take a look at some Bible verses that offer clues as to how to speak powerful, effective prayers. **Begin by reading John 14:14. What amazing promise does Jesus make?**

At first glance, it looks like Jesus is promising to give us anything we want, anything we ask. **Look a little closer at this verse and the additional verses listed. There are conditions and guidelines to the promise; what are they? Notice the context of each of these situations—what are the circumstances which prompted the instruction concerning prayer? Context affects the meaning of a statement.**

Matthew 18:19
John 15:1-11
(Note the context.)

John 14:13-14

John 15:16
Hebrews 5:7

Matthew 21:18-22

John 15:7

1 John 5:14-15

John 16:23-27

When Jesus says, "ask in My name," He does not mean tag the words "in the name of Jesus" onto the end of each prayer. There is nothing wrong with that phrase if you understand what you are saying; using it with no understanding of what you are actually saying, though, is pointless. Names in the Bible are very significant. They speak of a person's character qualities, who the person was on the inside. What we ask from God should line up with who Jesus is and what He demonstrated.

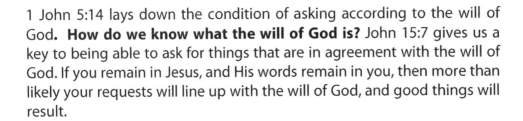

1 John 5:14 lays down the condition of asking according to the will of God. **How do we know what the will of God is?** John 15:7 gives us a key to being able to ask for things that are in agreement with the will of God. If you remain in Jesus, and His words remain in you, then more than likely your requests will line up with the will of God, and good things will result.

Summarize what you have learned about effective prayer.

I don't remember now who said it, but I recently heard, "Jesus didn't tell us what to do with unanswered prayer because He didn't expect there to be any." Father God offers us huge opportunity in prayer as we give ourselves fully to Him resulting in our thoughts and desires aligning with His and His with ours. Prayer is a powerful and effective tool God has given us for walking closely with Him. Let's not neglect it.

How do these references describe what our prayer life is to be like? What do they tell us about *when* we are to pray?

Psalm 5:3
Mark 1:35
Romans 12:12

1 Thessalonians 5:16-18

Luke 18:1
Colossians 4:12-13
Philippians 4:6

Ephesians 6:18

Matthew 5:44
Matthew 9:38
Luke 21:36
1 Timothy 2:1-4
1 Samuel 12:23

Ephesians 6:18 tells us to pray all kinds of prayers. **What are some of those kinds of prayers according to 1 Timothy 2:1?**

Use a dictionary to look up these four types of prayers. Notice how they are different from one another.

Ephesians 6:18 also tells us to pray in the Spirit. **Read the verse before it, Ephesians 6:17. What is the sword of the Spirit?**

Prayers that Paul prayed for believers:
Ephesians 1:15-21
Ephesians 3:14-19
Philippians 1:9-11
Colossians 1:9-12
2 Thess. 1:11-12
Philemon 1:4-6

One way to wield the sword of the Spirit is through prayer. Anytime you read a Scripture that speaks about your situation, pray it. Speak the words of the Scripture back to God in the form of a prayer. There is no surer way to praying the will of God than to pray with His very words.

Read Philippians 4:6. What are we to pray about?

For one more word of encouragement, look once again at Philippians 4. According to verse 7, what will happen for you as you begin to pray about everything?

Friend in Christ, there is so much more to learn about prayer. You can find dozens of books on the topic to learn more. Honestly, however, the best way to learn about prayer is by experience. You will discover the most about what prayer is and how it works simply by practicing. So just do it. Stand, sit, walk, kneel, lay with your face to the ground; whisper, holler, cry, laugh, sing, write—it doesn't matter how or where you pray— just that you pray always about everything.

4

Who is Jesus?

You've had an encounter with Jesus. You have entered a relationship making Him an intimate part of your life and your Lord. You've believed in Him for salvation and freedom from the power of sin. Who is this Jesus, and how is it that He can save you and, in fact, is the only one who can save you? Acts 4:12 leaves no doubt: "Salvation is found in no one else, for there is no other name under heaven given to mankind by which we must be saved." Let's see who the Bible says that Jesus is.

Take the time to look up each Scripture. Note the setting of the verse you are looking up. Who is speaking? Who are they speaking to? What is going on in this chapter of the Bible? It is important to pay attention to what surrounds the verse you are looking up because the parts before and after the passage help determine its meaning. This is called "context." All Scripture must be considered within its context to gain a true understanding of its meaning.

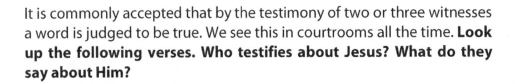

It is commonly accepted that by the testimony of two or three witnesses a word is judged to be true. We see this in courtrooms all the time. **Look up the following verses. Who testifies about Jesus? What do they say about Him?**

Matthew 16:13-17

John 1:29-34
John 20-30-31

Matthew 27:51-54 (This event happened at the moment Jesus died.)

Mark 3:11

Luke 8:27-32
Mark 1:21-27

Luke 1:26-35

Matthew 1:18-25

Luke 3:21-22

Acts 2:22
Luke 9:34-35

John 10:24-25, 30-33, 37-38

Luke 4:38-41
John 3:2
John 5:36-37
John 5:39

Okay. Okay. Many testified Jesus is the *Son* of God. But that doesn't make Jesus *God himself* does it? **Study the following Scriptures to find out. Note what each says about Jesus' relationship to God the Father.**

Matthew 1:23

John 14:20
John 17:21-23

John 5:17-20

Hebrews 1:1-3

John 10:30-38
John 20:28
Hebrews 1:8
Titus 2:13

John 10:30 (Jesus speaking)

Colossians 2:9

Here is a valuable Bible study instruction: whenever you read a passage, ask *who, what, when, where, why,* and *how* questions about what you are reading. For example, **read John 1:1-3 and John 1:14. List everything you learn about "the Word" from this passage. Look for answers to** *who* **the Word is,** *what* **it is and** *what* **it did,** *where* **the Word was and** *where* **it came from, and look for anything that answers** *when.*

Genesis 1

John 1:1-3, 14

Did you see that the term "Word" in these verses refers to Jesus? In verse 14 it says, "The Word became flesh and dwelt among us." Jesus is the one who became a man with flesh and lived among men on earth. **Read the verses again, this time substituting Jesus' name everywhere it says "Word."**

Another important Bible study tool is called cross-referencing. When you discover a truth in the Bible, check other verses to see if they confirm that truth or add more information. Cross-referencing or comparing Scripture with Scripture also helps bring understanding to a verse that is confusing or not completely clear.

Cross-referencing Colossians 1:15-19 confirms what we saw in John 1 and gives additional details about who Jesus is. Look closely at each verse and list what you learn. I know some of these ideas are difficult to understand. That's okay. Taking note of them even if you don't understand is still a valuable exercise. Ask Holy Spirit to expand your understanding, to open the eyes of your heart, and to be your teacher.

1:15

John 1:3-5
Romans 1136

1:16

1:17

1:18

1:19

Take a few minutes to ponder the immenseness of who Apostle Paul describes Jesus to be. The phrase in verse 19 "all his fullness dwell in him" means that all God is filled with is also in Jesus—everything God is, Jesus is.

Wait a minute. I thought Christianity is based on the idea that there is only one God. How can Jesus be God *and* God be God? And, in case you didn't know, the Holy Spirit, whom we have talked about in previous lessons, is also God.

"Trinity" is the word we use to describe our three-in-one God. Deuteronomy 6:4 says, "Hear, O Israel: The Lord our God, the Lord is one." Yet, throughout Scripture we see God the Father, God the Son, and God the Holy Spirit spoken of separately. If you want to, read the passages listed in the center column and look for clues showing that the Father, Son, and Spirit indeed are three, yet they are one. If you still don't understand this concept, that's okay. Sometimes we choose to embrace the mystery of who God is by faith—we just believe.

Our focus for this lesson, though, is to search out who Jesus is and how it is that we can trust Him for forgiveness and freedom from sin. **According to Isaiah 43:10-11, 25 who forgives sins? Note who is speaking in this passage.**

About the Trinity:
Genesis 1:26-27
(note the plural and singular words)

Isaiah 43:10-11
Isaiah 44:6
Isaiah 45:18

Malachi 2:10
(compare this to Genesis1:26-27)

Matthew 28:19
John 16:7-15
(Note how all three work together.)

John 17:21
1 Corinthians 8::4-6
James 2:19

Hebrews 1:8
Titus 2:13
John 1:1
John 20:28

In Mark 2:5-12, the teachers of the law were upset. Why?

What do we learn about Jesus in this passage?

What does Jesus say about himself in the following passages?

John 8:23-30
John 10:9-14

John 5:16-18

John 5:17-23
John 14:1
John 14:7-11

John 14:6

What about you? What do you believe about Jesus? According to what you believe, what is true of you?

Psalm 103:1-22
1 John 2:21-24

1 John 4:13-15

Romans 10:9-10

Acts 16:30-31

John 3:18

John 3:36

Friend in Christ, what you believe about Jesus is a critical ingredient in your spiritual life. If you believe Jesus is indeed who He says He is and have called upon Him for salvation, you are indeed saved. There is no other name given among men by which we must be saved. You are saved; live like it; rejoice in it. Nothing can take this away from you.

Thank you for being diligent to study God's Word and to find out for yourself what the truth is. I know the Word is strength and life to you because it is to me also. Keep up the good work.

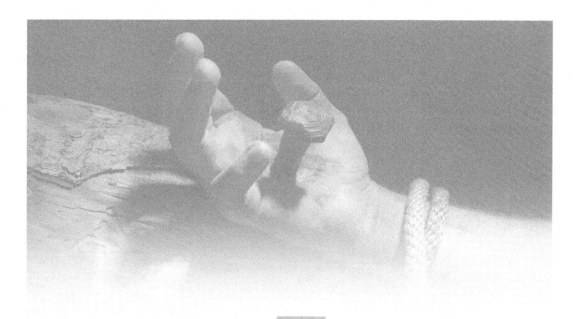

5

Why Did Jesus Have to Die?

When God makes a promise, you can count on Him to keep it. Today, we will look at the promise of salvation and eternal life God made to mankind and why it required the life of His son to keep that promise.

Did you pray? Ask God to give you understanding as you study today.

Before we dive into this lesson's topic, let's set a foundation of the character of God. When someone's good character is a sure thing, we can know that everything that person does stems from that character. Then, even when we don't understand a particular action that person takes, we can still trust, knowing his or her character is intact.

Psalm 103:1-18 beautifully describes God's character. **How do these verses describe what God is like? Take some time to meditate on each of these astounding attributes.**

Nehemiah 9:17 (also, the entire chapter) Exodus 34:6-7

Look at 1 John 4:16. You might already know that God loves you, but this verse reveals something deeper about that love. More specifically, it tells you something important about the God who loves. **What does this verse reveal about God?**

Look back a few verses at 1 John 4:9-10. How did God show His love for us?

Read John 3:16-17. Again, why did God send His Son Jesus? What does this show you about His intentions toward mankind?

Psalm 36:5-6
1 John 4:10

Are you getting the idea that God *is* love and everything He does is founded in love? He loves you and wants you to be in relationship with Himself. Father, Son, and Holy Spirit together were willing to go to all extremes to bring you into that relationship and into the salvation John 3 speaks of.

But why did this love and relationship cost Jesus His life? Why the cross? Let's start at the beginning.

Genesis 2 & 3
Genesis 2:7
John 20:22

At the creation of the world and everything in it, God looked at what He made and said, "It is very good." He had formed man (male and female) out of the dust of the earth, breathed life into them, and placed them in the Garden of Eden, a place where heaven and earth were one. Adam and Eve walked in close relationship with God in the Garden. The humans were given the commission to partner with God in ruling over

Romans 8:32
1 Peter 1:3
Matthew 10:8

all created things on the earth. Everything in the Garden was freely given to them to enjoy except the fruit of the "Tree of the Knowledge of Good and Evil" which was in the middle of the garden. This one tree they were told not to eat from, and it sat right alongside of the "Tree of Life" which they enjoyed unhindered access to..

Genesis 2:4-17

In Genesis 2:16-17, what did God say would happen if they ate the fruit of that one forbidden tree?

-James 1:13-17
Deuteronomy
30:19-20

Did God set man up for failure by putting this troublesome tree in His glorious garden? No. God set man up for freedom—freedom to choose to love Him in return through trust and obedience. Without this free will, man was merely a puppet to do God's will, and true reciprocal relationship could not exist. The choice is simple: life or death. God created the earth to be filled with life and order. Choosing to follow Him is to choose life. To step outside of God is to choose to step into death and disorder—not because God will punish you, but because it is the natural consequence and the only other option.

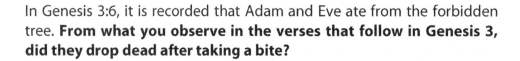

In Genesis 3:6, it is recorded that Adam and Eve ate from the forbidden tree. **From what you observe in the verses that follow in Genesis 3, did they drop dead after taking a bite?**

Is God a liar then? No. The original Hebrew word in this verse could be literally translated "dying you will die" indicating that their eating of that fruit introduced deterioration into their lives. How so? Well, one obvious answer is that because of their choice, Adam and Eve had to leave the Garden of Eden. Their access to the Tree of Life directly depended on their choice regarding the Tree of the Knowledge of Good and Evil. Outside of the Garden, Adam eventually died at age 930; over the centuries, the expected lifespan of man shortened to under 100 years. It appears there was relational and spiritual death introduced as well that then became a reality for all mankind.

Genesis 3:22-24

Genesis 5:5

Look at Ephesians 2:1-5. How does it describe people who are separated from God?

Luke 15:24
Romans 5:12-21
Romans 7:9-11

You might ask, if Adam and Eve had no knowledge of good and evil, how could it be wrong for them to eat from the forbidden tree? It's not that they had no knowledge; they walked with God in the Garden; of course, He was teaching them what they needed to know in order to rule and subdue the earth. Man's relationship with God was based on faith and love. It was out of that relationship that Adam and Eve were to choose to obey God. It wasn't about keeping knowledge from them; it was about love and recognizing God as the definer of good and evil. 1 John 5:3 says, "This is love for God: to obey His commands." Because of the tree, man was able to *choose* to obey God and trust His defining of good and evil. Freewill became the test of true love. Man failed the test, choosing to obey Satan rather than God and thus becoming a slave to sin.

John 14:15

Luke 4:6-7

Romans 6:16-18

After Adam and Eve listened to the lie of the serpent and chose sin, they then saw themselves and each other differently. Where they had been comfortable to be open and vulnerable without fear, they now saw themselves as naked and ashamed. Now fearful, they tried to hide themselves from each other with fig leaves while hiding among the bushes from God whom they had walked freely with from the beginning.

God didn't change the day Adam and Eve sinned. He didn't become an angry, disappointed God. He came to the garden to be with Adam and Eve that day just as He always did. It was man who had changed. As we've already said, the love of the Father for all mankind would not allow sin to keep us from Him. We are only separated from God when we choose to hide ourselves from Him.

What did God do for Adam and Eve in Genesis 3:21?

Hebrews 9:22
Leviticus 16:34
Leviticus 17:11

Does that sound like tender loving care to you? It does to me, though truly it was at the cost of the shedding of blood. Since the beginning, blood was necessary to cover the sin of man. Life is in the blood; the shedding of blood reminds us that the cost of sin is death.

Exodus 30:10
Hebrews 9:1-7

Romans 5:12-21

In time, when God established a covenant with Moses, which included the Ten Commandments. He set up a system of sacrificing perfect lambs and bulls so that each year men would be cleansed of sin committed, and the penalty of death would be satisfied for a season. These sacrifices are described in the books of Exodus and Leviticus. This covenant is also called the "Law." While explaining the scope and purpose of this system that is puzzling to the modern mind is far beyond the ability of this author and this book, let's see if we can walk through enough to answer our question, "Why did Jesus have to die?"

Romans 8:3-4
Romans 3:20
Hebrews 9:12-14
Hebrews 10:1-18

Read Hebrews 10:1-4. Even though the lambs used were spotless, what was the problem with animal sacrifice?

What purpose did animal sacrifice actually serve?

Look at Hebrews chapter 9. Take the time to read this entire chapter in a simplified version of the Bible like the New Living Translation or The Message Bible. This will help clarify its meaning.

According to Hebrews 9:22-23, why was it necessary for God to give His son as a sacrifice?

Animal sacrifice wasn't enough. There had to be a more perfect sacrifice. Only the blood of a sinless man could recover what was lost by man in the Garden of Eden that day.

Romans 5:12-20

Are there any sinless men? Could someone else have made the sacrifice?

Romans 3:23

1 John 1:8
Colossians 2:13-15

Romans 5:12

Look at Galatians 4:4-5. When the time was right, what did God do? Why?

Read Luke 1:31, 34-35. How was Jesus conceived? Did He have the seed of Adam passed on to Him?

Jesus was the only man besides Adam who was born without the corruption of sin and death within Him. He now has the same choice that Adam had in the garden—to sin or not to sin. The same choice that brought sin into the world can now be used to stop the power of sin and death, if indeed the man Jesus can live a sinless life on this earth.

Did He do it? Did Jesus, the Son of God, live on earth as any other man? Did He do it without sin? List what the following verses say about Him.

2 Corinthians 5:21
1 Peter 1:18-20
1 Peter 2:21-24
1 John 3:5
Luke 4:1-14

Philippians 2:6-8

Hebrews 2:17-18

Hebrews 4:15

Go back to the passage in Hebrews 10:1-4. How does verse 1 describe the Law also known as the first covenant?

What was the good thing to come that the Law was foreshadowing? What was to be the ultimate sacrificial offering? Look to Hebrews 10:9-18 for the answer. The pronoun "he" in these verses is referring to Jesus.

Will a sacrifice ever be needed again? Notice the words in this passage that express time. Write down what they say.

Hebrews 7:22-28
1 Peter 3:18-22

verse 10 (once)

verse 11 (never)

verse 12-13 (for all time)

verse 14 (forever)

verse 15-18 (no longer)

Jesus gave His life in exchange for ours, but was that the end of the story? **What happened after Jesus' death and burial?**

Matthew 12:40
Matthew 16:21
Acts 10:39-41
1 Corinthians 15:1-8
Hebrews 1:3-4

Mark 16:1-14

Where is Jesus now?

Acts 1:9-11
Psalm 110:1
1 Peter 3:21-22

Galatians 2:20
Ephesians 3:16-19
1 John 3:24

Ephesians 1:20-21

John 14:29-20, 23

What is Jesus doing now?

Romans 8:34

Ephesians 1:22-23

Revelation 3:7
Isaiah 25:8
1 Corinthians 15:25
Colossians 1:18

John 17:25-26

Because He is risen, what does He now hold?

1 Corinthians 15:26

Revelation 1:17-18

How does Jesus' death and resurrection affect you, the believer? What has happened to your old self and why?

Galatians 5:24
Colossians 2:13-14

Romans 5:17-19

Galatians 2:20

Romans 6:3-8

What do you think? Can you see that Jesus' astounding act of love through the cross was what Father, Son, and Holy Spirit together were willing to do for the sake of bringing mankind into intimate relationship with Himself?

Look at Ephesians 3:12 and think back to what we saw in the Garden of Eden when sin first entered the life of man. What has now been restored to us?

It is finished, friend in Christ. Through His sacrifice, Jesus has conquered death and sin's hold on those who choose Him. He opened a new and better way to unhindered relationship with God that provides abundant life here on earth as well as the promise of eternal life after physical death. Because Jesus came to earth as a man, lived a sinless life, died on the cross, rose from the dead and now sits at the right hand of the Father, every human being who believes is now included in that God relationship along with all its benefits. There is but one thing for you to do in order to receive God's promised salvation, fellowship with God, and eternal life—that is to believe in Jesus Christ.

Just as it did for Adam and Eve in the beginning, this wonderful relationship with God carries responsibilities. Your presence here on earth as a new creation is important. Now that you are justified and made righteous, what will your life look like? We'll talk about that in the final two chapters.

6
How Then Should We Live?

In John 19:30, Jesus said, "It is finished!" Then he bowed his head and released his spirit. Today we will look at what is finished, what that actually means to you and me, and how we live out this new Christian life now because of it.

First, let's look at exactly what was finished. **In the following verses, look for the reason Jesus came. Remember that it has already been accomplished and think of each of these as personal victories for your own life.**

1 Timothy 1:15

1 John 3:5

1 John 3:8

Matthew 20:28

Luke 4:18-19

John 3:17
Luke 19:10
Colossians 2:13-15
1 John 4:9-10
John 10:7-18

John 17 (Jesus'
prayer expresses His
final desires.)

John 10:10

Moments before He died, Jesus said, "It is finished." Did He do what He came to do? Do you think this list of reasons for which He came was accomplished? How does that affect your life?

John 17:4

Romans chapter 6 has some pretty exciting news and instructions concerning what the finished work of the cross has accomplished in you. Romans 6:3-5 tells us that if we believe in Jesus then we also identify with his death. In other words, we, too, have "died," and, just as Christ was raised from the dead, we too may live a new life. All that Jesus accomplished through the cross belongs to every believer.

Read Romans 6:6-7. What happened to your old self and why?

2 Corinthians 5:14-17

Galatians 2:20

1 Peter 2:24

According to the English dictionary, what is a slave?

Romans 8:2

What does it mean to be a slave to sin?

According to Romans 6:7, are you, as a believer in Jesus Christ, in bondage to sin?

Psalm 119:104

Romans 6 makes it so clear that believers have been set free from sin. Yet so many have real struggles living free from sin. Why? The writer of Romans asks the same question in verse 2, "We died to sin, how can we live in it any longer?" Right after he asks the question, he offers an answer. **See Romans 6:2-3.** Paul suggests that the reason we struggle must be because there is something important we do not yet know or understand.

Some of us are not free from the pattern of sin in our lives even though we are born again because we do not truly know and believe that we have been baptized into Christ's death—that our old selves have died.

The New Testament was originally written in the Greek language. The phrase "don't you know" in Romans 6:3 in the Greek dictionary has three meanings. Those who continue to act as slaves to sin either 1) don't know the truth that they have died with Christ, 2) don't understand the implications of this truth, or 3) aren't making good use of this truth.

1 Peter 1:14-19
Romans 12:2

Do you live as a slave to sin? If so, do any of these definitions apply to you and the way you view sin in your life? What needs to change in order for you to live free?

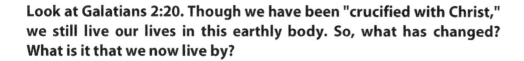

Look at Galatians 2:20. Though we have been "crucified with Christ," we still live our lives in this earthly body. So, what has changed? What is it that we now live by?

To be free from sin, you must first believe that the work Christ did on the cross was complete, that your old man no longer lives, and that sin no longer holds any power over you. It is finished. Your old man isn't just sleeping or taking a vacation or even in the process of dying. Your old nature isn't "mostly dead." You are dead to sin, and it is Christ who now lives in you.

Ezekiel 11:19-20
Ezekiel 36:26-27

2 Corinthians 5:17, 22

How? In real life—in this human body with all its difficult human circumstances—how do I actually live this way? **Read Romans 6:8-13. There are several instructions given to the believer who wants to live for God. What are they?**

Verse 11

Galatians 5:1

Galatians 5:16-25

Verse 12

Verse 13

   1)

   2)

   3)

Ephesians 4:21-32

Proverbs 3:5-6

Romans 8:5-7

Romans 12:2

2 Corinthians 11:3

Do you recognize that being able to do the things listed in Romans 6 begins with your thought patterns and belief system? When you believe that Christ has won your victory over sin—it is finished—then sin will have no power over you.

Colossians 3 gives very practical help in living out this new life to God. **Look carefully for any instructions given. List them.** You will see things you should put off and things you should put on. There will be instructions regarding your attitude and guidance for your actions. The rest of this page is left blank for you to do this thoroughly.

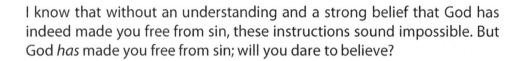

I know that without an understanding and a strong belief that God has indeed made you free from sin, these instructions sound impossible. But God *has* made you free from sin; will you dare to believe?

Colossians 3:5 offers a key to living free— "put to death what belongs to your earthly nature." Notice it does not say put to death the old nature— your old nature is already dead—but put to death what belongs to the old nature.

How can a mere man do this? He can't. **Read Romans 8:12-13. How are the misdeeds of the body put to death? Who helps you?**

Galatians 5:19-21
Galatians 6:8
Romans 8:2
Titus 2:11-12

Remember what we learned about Holy Spirit in an earlier lesson? He is your teacher, helper, comforter. He is your provider of understanding, strength, and wisdom for a holy life. Lean into Holy Spirit. You are not alone.

Does all this talk of being free from sin mean that a true Christian never sins? Let's look at two Scriptures before coming to a conclusion on this question. Write them out.

Psalm 32:5

1 John 1:9

Romans 12:2

1 John 3:6

1 John 2:1-2

Romans 5:3-5

At first it seems that the author of First John cannot make up his mind—is one who commits sin a friend of Christ or not? However, if you look closely at the words, you will see a difference in the sin mentioned in these two verses. The sin spoken of in 3:6 is a continuous or repeated action, a lifestyle of sin. The sin in 2:1 is an isolated action. The person in 2:1 might make a wrong choice that leads to sin, but he quickly turns to Christ for forgiveness and continues to pursue what is right.

Through the cross of Christ, believers have been given the power to live a life free from the compulsion to sin, but when we sometimes choose sin anyway, Jesus is there for us, standing in His own righteousness before the Father on our behalf.

John 16:33

Jesus said you will have trials and temptations in your life. There is a spiritual battle going on, but it is important for you to understand who or what the fight is against. **According to Ephesians 6:12, what is our struggle with?**

What is our struggle not with?

If our struggle is not against flesh and blood, do you think that includes your own? When Jesus said, "It is finished," was it enough to cover your sin? Or is your temptation bigger than the cross? I know these are strong words and, if you are struggling with sin, they may seem unkind, but this is GOOD NEWS!

James 4:7

What is the good news concerning this spiritual battle according to John 16:33 and 1 John 4:4?

As you are hopefully well aware by now, more good news is that you don't have to walk this holy life alone nor in your own strength. Jesus accomplished it on the cross and gave us the Holy Spirit who is living in us as our constant companion, teaching us God's ways and helping us to walk rightly.

Read 2 Peter 1:3-4. What else have you been given? Where does it come from?

2 Corinthians 12:9
Romans 8:32

Pursue knowing Jesus. Know Him through the Scriptures and through constant awareness of His presence in your life. The knowledge of Him opens up everything you need for a godly life, all of which has already been given to you. As you get to know and understand His ways, His glory, and His excellence, you step into the promises He has made concerning your salvation, abundant life on earth, and eternal life in the new heaven and new earth (see 2 Peter 3:13).

Isaiah 65:17-25
Revelation 21:1-4

According to 2 Peter 1:4, what are God's promises making way for you to do?

What promises are made to you in 1 Corinthians 10:13?

Psalm 103:13-14

Genesis 4:7-8

What is that way out? **Look up the following verses for three strategies to consider.**

1. 1 Timothy 6:11, 2 Timothy 2:22 (What is the two-part common strategy repeated in both of these verses?)

1 Corinthians 10:12
2 Corinthians 10:5

2. Ephesians 6:11, 13

3. James 4:7-8

We have to be on guard against temptations. Remain aware of the devil's schemes and on the lookout for them without being consumed by fear because, as we already know, greater is He who is in us than he who is in the world. Sometimes we need to just plain run from temptation like Timothy was told. Sometimes we use the tactic of drawing near to God in order to resist the devil, and he is the one who runs. Sometimes we stubbornly stand our ground. There is always a way out; you always have a choice.

James 1:12-16
Genesis 4:7

According to James 1:2-4, why would God allow you to be tempted in the first place?

Luke 22::31-32
Romans 8:28-29
Romans 8:38-39
Lamentations 3:21-23
Titus 2:11-14

Every time you choose right in the face of temptation (and trust in the Holy Spirit to help you follow through on that choice), you are becoming more like Jesus. Though God is not the tempter (see James 1:13), He obligates these difficult situations to work for your good in part by providing opportunities for you to grow in Christ. He rewards those who hold fast to their faith with a crown of life (see James 1:12).

If you do find yourself in a struggle with sin (or anything for that matter), what does Hebrews 4:16 say you can do about it?

Ephesians 6:13
1 Peter 5:8-10

Mercy is God's kindness toward the afflicted combined with His desire to help them. Grace is different. Grace is God's holy influence upon our hearts, turning them to Christ. Through Grace, God divinely kindles our hearts to exercise faith and good choices. Yet, the choice is still ours to make.

James 4:6
1 Peter 5:5

Friend in Christ, there are some big promises we've looked at in this lesson, but I assure you they are truth. It is in believing that God has indeed freed you that you will find freedom.

I want you to see one more important promise that God has made to you in His Word. Hear Philippians 1:6, "He who began a good work in you will carry it on to completion until the day of Christ Jesus." Let the Holy Spirit burn this thought into your heart and mind so that you will know that though there may be challenges, the outcome of your walk with Christ need never be uncertain.

7

Welcome To the Family

There is no doubt that you are now a new creation since you believed in Christ. Everything has changed. Something else has happened to you as well. You have been brought into the family of God. But what does that mean? This lesson is a little longer than the previous ones. Perhaps because it is a topic I am passionate about. Don't rush through it. We are not in a hurry to be done.

Let's start with a basic question. Aren't all humans God's children? Or is it only the Jewish people who are God's family? How do I know if I am part of God's family? Though the Lord had set apart the nation of Israel in the time of Abraham to forever be His own people, He did so in order that Israel would draw all nations to Him. The truth is that He has always been near to anyone who would call upon His name (Psalm 145:18).

Then later, Jesus' coming, death, and resurrection sealed a new covenant between God and man. Romans 10 tells us there is now no distinction between Jew and Gentile (everyone who is not a Jew) and that anyone who believes on the name of Jesus will be saved. In other words, we believing gentiles have been adopted.

How do you know that *you* are part of God's family? According to these verses, to whom was given the right to be called children of God?

Romans 8:14-17

John 1:10-13

Galatians 3:26-29

According to Ephesians 1:4-5, what is God's motivation for adopting you as His child?

1 John 1:3

Luke 12:32

v. 4

v.5

v.5

First Timothy 2:4 tells us it is God's desire for all men to be saved, to be part of his family. Yet, He has given us the choice. We can receive Jesus and believe in His name, thus becoming a child of God. Or, we can choose not to. **Look again at John 1:12. According to this verse, do *you* have the right to be called a son or daughter of God? How do you feel about that?**

Ezekiel 18:23, 32
Romans 10:13
2 Peter 3:9

Deuteronomy 30:19-20
Joshua 24:15

Psalm 89:14
Psalm 145:17
Matthew 7:11
James 1:5

Almighty God, creator of heaven and earth, calls Himself your Father. Understand that He is Father in every good and perfect sense of the word. If your experience with a human father has not been good, ask the Holy Spirit to show you the goodness of your heavenly Father so that you can see Him as He truly is.

Being part of God's family has its privileges and also its responsibilities. Obviously, the Bible is packed from cover to cover with truths and instructions regarding being a child of God. We will pull out only a few of them just to help you grasp the largeness of what you have entered into and so that you will begin to know God's heart toward His family.

First, let's look at the benefits you receive as a legally adopted child of God.

What are some of the things you can expect to receive from Father God as His child according to these passages?

Luke 11:9-13
Matthew 6:4, 6, 18
James 1:17

1 John 3:1

Psalm 103:13

Matthew 7:7-11

Another benefit is that you receive the family likeness. **What is happening to you according to these verses?**

Romans 12:2-3
Colossians 3:9-10

1 John 3:2
1 John 4:16-17
Ephesians 5:1
Luke 6:40

2 Corinthians 3:18

Romans 8:29-30

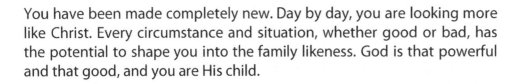

You have been made completely new. Day by day, you are looking more like Christ. Every circumstance and situation, whether good or bad, has the potential to shape you into the family likeness. God is that powerful and that good, and you are His child.

Read more of this passage in Romans 8. Review Romans 8:28-39 in several different versions of the Bible. This is the family you belong to. This is the powerful and passionate Father who has called you His own. His love runs deep. His passion for you is fierce. As you are being made like Christ, there is no circumstance, situation, or entity that can get in the way of nor lessen His love for you. All things work for good.

According to Galatians 4:7, as a member of the family of God, what else are you?

Romans 8:17
1 Corinthians 2:9
1 Peter 1:3-5

What is an heir? Use a dictionary to look up the definition of this word.

What have we inherited?

1 Corinthians 6:9-11

Matthew 19:29

Matthew 25:34

What should be our attitude toward our inheritance?

Colossians 3:23-24, 17

The entire chapter of
Colossians 3 adds to
this thought.

Our inheritance of eternal life is so important to Father God that He gave us the Holy Spirit as a deposit to ensure its reality. This is not something

Ephesians 1:13-14

we can take for granted nor carry an entitlement attitude about. What a precious and costly thing Father has promised to us. We can honor and respect our inheritance with our actions and the heart motivations behind them.

As you continue to learn as a Christian, you will discover an unlimited pool of blessings that come from being a part of the family of God. His promises to us are immense. May you enjoy the journey of discovering all that is yours in Christ. You will also discover that there are some responsibilities that come with being part of the family.

If we who have turned to Jesus as Savior are the children of God, what is our relationship to one another?

Ephesians 5:23

Ephesians 3:6

Romans 8:29
Matthew 12:47-50

Hebrews 2:11

We are family, and families are meant to be together. We truly need one another. **List the four instructions found in Hebrews 10:23-25. What do you learn from them?**

v.23

v.24

v.25

Acts 11:26

v.25

What was Paul praying for in Romans 1:9-10?

What was he hoping this would accomplish according to Romans 1:11-12?

The book of Acts in the Bible tells the story of the Church that developed after Jesus' death. **What are some of the things these believers did? Also notice the way their hearts were affected by these activities.**

Acts 20:20-21
Colossians 3:16-17
James 5:14

Acts 2:41-47

Did you know Jesus went to church often? The books of Matthew, Mark, Luke, and John—which are the Bible books that tell the story of Jesus' time on earth—repeatedly speak of Jesus being at the temple, even every day. Paul, the apostle who wrote most of the New Testament, was also in the temple quite often. Believers also met together in homes, in church buildings, and even outdoors throughout the New Testament.

Matthew 21:23
Matthew 26:55
Mark 11:27
Mark 12:41
Luke 20:1
Luke 21:37
John 10:23
John 18:21

In 1 Corinthians 14:26, what is Paul's instruction to the Church? What is the desired effect of obeying this instruction?

Acts 5:42
Acts 16:13
1 Corinthians 16:19

"Built up" in this verse means "the act of one who promotes another's growth in Christian wisdom, in devotion to God, in happiness, and in holiness." That is our job when we are gathered together as a church. We don't come only to receive something from the leader. I have something

Romans 14:19
1 Corinthians 10:23-24

to build you up; you have something to build me up. As Paul said in Romans 1:12, we come together for a mutual exchange that encourages each other's faith.

Most of us have experienced the fact that when family gets together, it is not always encouraging. Sometimes there is misconduct and conflicts within family. We can see throughout the Bible that the Church certainly isn't perfect either. There are folks who are not behaving in godly ways, and there are sometimes divisions among believers. Scripture does give instruction and solutions for these matters, some of which we will discuss later in this chapter.

For now, I want us to see our need for one another and develop a value for one another as one family of God. **What simile does Romans 12:4-5 use to describe our relationship to one another?**

1 Corinthians
10:16-17

Does this passage say that we are all alike or must all become alike? What is the instruction in verse 6-8?

1 Corinthians 12:4-11
1 Corinthians 7:7
Ephesians 4:4-7

1 Corinthians 12:12-27 expresses this same idea in more detail. **What is the main message of this Scripture passage?**

According to Colossians 1:18, who is the head of this metaphorical body? What is another name for the body?

We, the individual members of the body of Christ, make up the Church. Some believers never understand their own value to the Church, the family of God, and so much time and energy is wasted in comparing ourselves to one another resulting in our feeling less than enough or in thinking of ourselves more highly than we should. You have a viable role in the family. Go ahead and step up to it, allow yourself to grow into it, and enjoy being part of the family. If you don't know yet if you are an "arm" or a "leg" or an "internal organ," stay close. Pursue understanding of who God is and the things He cares about. Listen to those with more experience. Listen to your heart. Pay attention to the things that give you joy or stir your passion. These are clues that will lead to understanding your part in the body of Christ. In the meantime, just jump in. Pursue knowing Christ and knowing other believers.

Would you like to know how Jesus feels about His Church? You should already know beyond doubt that He loves you as an individual. We have learned that the individuals who are born again together make up the family of God, also known as the body of Christ, also known as the Church. **Ephesians 5:22-32 gives instructions to husbands and wives, but read between the lines to see what this passage says about Jesus and the Church. Note what He does for the Church and how the Church is to respond.**

Jesus told His disciples that they were to love and value one another just as He loved them. **How important is our love for one another to Father?**

John 15:9-14

John 13:34-35

John 13:12-15
1 John 2:8-10
1 John 3:14-16

1 John 3:10-11

The Word has much, much more to say about the responsibility brothers and sisters in Christ have toward one another. Let's look at just a few of the things God cares about amongst His family.

Romans 12:9 tells us love must be sincere. Then the verses following describe what sincere love looks like. **List the specific ways we are to relate to one another according to Romans 12:10-18.**

What do you learn in Galatians 6:9-10 about how we are to treat one another? Look for answers to What we are to do. When? To Whom? What will be the result?

What warning is given in Galatians 5:14-15?

What do you think "biting and devouring" each other means?

The Bible dictionary says biting means "to wound the soul; to tear someone to pieces violently by rebuking or disgracing them." Devouring is "to ruin or consume someone's mental and physical strength by strong emotion."

Rather than hurting each other as in Galatians 5:15, what can we do to help a brother or sister with whom we are having a problem? What is to be your state of mind and heart in this situation?

Romans 14:1
Romans 15:1
James 5:19-20

Isaiah 35:3-4
Matthew 18:15-17
Luke 15:11-32

Galatians 6:1-3

What caution is also mentioned in Galatians 6:1? How do you protect yourself according to this verse?

What else are we to do for one another according to Colossians 3:12-13?

Verses 14 and 15 remind us of the tools we need in order to respond in this way to one another. What are the instructions in these two verses?

As you can see, there is a lot involved in being a member of God's family. It is important to remember that the grace of God and the Holy Spirit in you are what make it possible for you to live this way toward Christ and toward one another. If we could do these things on our own, Jesus would not have needed to die. Ask Holy Spirit to help you, and receive the grace that is freely given to you.

Additional instructions
for believers toward
one another:
Mark 9:50
John 13:14
John 13:34
Romans 12:10
Romans 12:16
Romans 13:8
Romans 14:10-21
Romans 15:5-7
Romans 15:14
Romans 16:16
1 Corinthians 11:33
1 Corinthians 16:20
Galatians 5:13-15
Galatians 5:26
Galatians 6:1-2
Ephesians 4:32
Ephesians 5:19-21
Philippians 2:3
Colossians 3:9
Colossians 3;12-17
1 Thessalonians 3:12
1 Thessalonians 4:18
Hebrews 3:12-13
Hebrews 10:24-25
James 2:15-16
James 4:11
James 5:9, 16
1 Peter 1:22
1 Peter 3:8
1 Peter 4:8-10
1 Peter 5;5
1 John

There are still many more verses on the subject of our relationship with one another. If you want to know more, you can look up the verses listed in the reference column on the right. Note the many instructions given to us concerning our behavior and attitude toward others.

Friend in Christ, Jesus said the greatest commandment is to love God with all your heart, soul, strength, and mind (Matthew 22:37-40). That's it. That is the greatest thing you can do with your Christian life—love God fervently. Jesus also said the second greatest commandment is like it— love each other. May Second Thessalonians 1:3 be true of you as it says, "We ought always to thank God for you brothers, and rightly so, because your faith is growing more and more, and the love every one of you has for each other is increasing."

Welcome to the family!

Until Next Time…

Thank you for taking this journey through the Scriptures to understand what really just happened to you when you called on the name of the Lord. Our spiritual enemy, the devil, would love for you to be confused or uncertain of your salvation. But, as you have seen, through our knowledge of Christ, we have everything we need to live a godly life here on earth and a glorious eternity in heaven.

The kingdom of God is massive, and the truths and experiences for you to discover about it are innumerable. Continue to press in to know Him. God himself invites you into this discovery. Draw close to Him, and He will draw close to you. Abide in Him, and He will abide in you. He will never leave you nor forsake you.

Enjoy the journey, friend in Christ.

Regina McCollam

Made in the USA
Middletown, DE
03 June 2023

31869487R00040